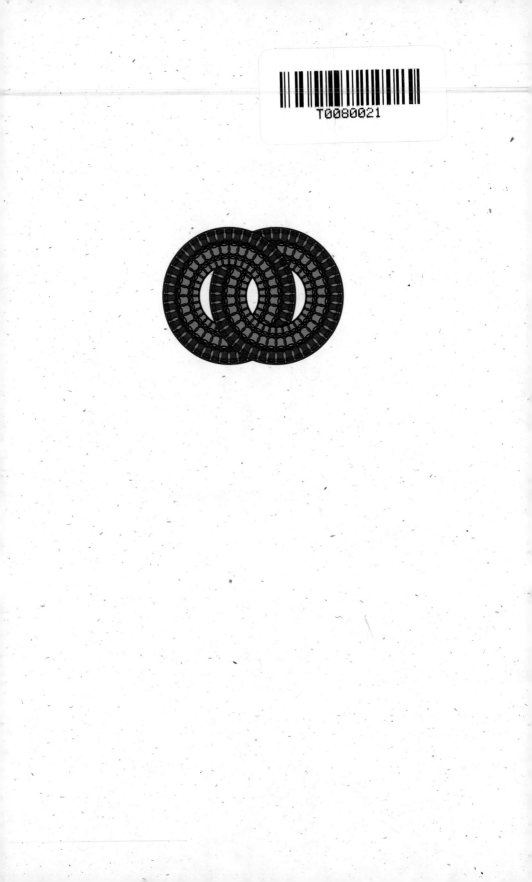

WORKS

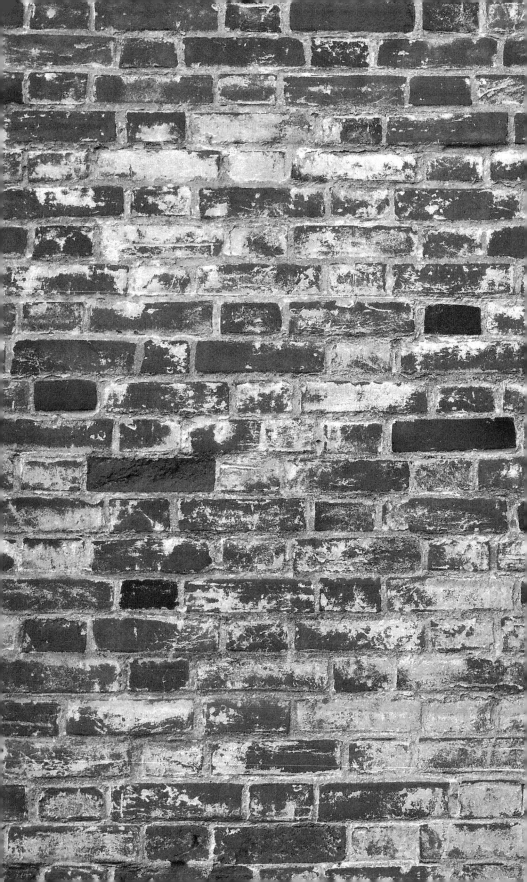

WORKS

DANNY SHOT

CavanKerry ◈ Press LTD.

CavanKerry Press Ltd.
Fort Lee, New Jersey
www.cavankerrypress.org

Publisher's Cataloging-In-Publication Data
(Prepared by The Donohue Group, Inc.)
Names: Shot, Danny.
Title: Works / Danny Shot.
Description: First edition. | Fort Lee, New Jersey : CavanKerry Press Ltd., 2018.
Identifiers: ISBN 9781933880655
Subjects: LCSH: Shot, Danny—Poetry. | New Jersey—Poetry. | New York (N.Y.)—
    Poetry. | High school teaching—Poetry. | Adult children of immigrants—
    United States—Poetry.
Classification: LCC PS3569.H5977 W67 2018 | DDC 811/.54—dc23

Cover photograph: "Jefferson Avenue–Camden NJ" by Blake Bolinger
Author photo by John Dalton
Cover and interior text design by Ryan Scheife, Mayfly Design
First Edition 2018, Printed in the United States of America

FLORENZ EISMAN
Memorial Series
CavanKerry ⊛ Press

CavanKerry Press is proud to present the second book in the Florenz Eisman Memorial Series—fine collections by New Jersey poets, notable or emerging. A gifted poet and great lover of poetry herself, Florenz was CavanKerry's Managing Editor from its inception in 2000 until her passing in 2013. The publisher's partner in establishing the press, her ideas and intelligence were a great source of inspiration for writers and staff alike as were her quick wit and signature red lipstick.

CavanKerry Press is grateful for the support it receives from the New Jersey State Council on the Arts.

For Caroline, Casey, Levi, and Carol . . . simply because

everybody wants you to be just like them
well, I try my best to be just like I am

—BOB DYLAN, "MAGGIE'S FARM"

Contents

IV

V

WORKS

Foreword

As a founder and editor of the long-running *Long Shot* literary magazine, as an organizer of countless poetry readings over decades, and as the current Poet-in-Residence at the Hoboken Historical Museum, Danny Shot has been one of New Jersey's best poets and best promoters of poetry for over thirty-five years now. The publication of Danny's first full-length book of poems is therefore a cause for celebration in the literary world. And with the 2016 disastrous election of Donald Trump, we need reasons to celebrate as much as ever!

For many years, *Long Shot* magazine was promoted as "writing for the real world," and that description perfectly fits Danny's own poetry. Or, even better, writing for, *and from,* the real world. For a small state, New Jersey has had a long and remarkable impact on the American poetry world, producing an extraordinary number of influential poets—beginning with Walt Whitman and moving on to William Carlos Williams, Allen Ginsberg, Alicia Ostriker, Amiri Baraka, Anne Waldman, Herschel Silverman, Nancy Mercado, Joel Lewis, Cheryl Clarke, Joe Weil, Maria Mazziotti Gillan, Reg E. Gaines, Bruce Springsteen, Patti Smith, and many more. Among the traits all these writers share have been a courage to speak one's mind, a commitment to confront pressing social issues, and a desire to use poetry to reach both the heads and hearts of readers. With the publication of this new book, Danny takes his rightful place within the distinguished tradition of New Jersey poets.

While some schools of contemporary American poetry can sometimes read like jigsaw puzzles that might take dedicated readers hours or weeks to put together, Danny's poetry is unwavering in its desire to communicate. In addition to being influenced by writers like Walt Whitman, the poets of the Beat Generation, Patti Smith, Pedro Pietri, and Charles

Bukowski, Danny's aesthetic preference for an accessible style can also be traced to the fact that he has been a dedicated teacher in New York City public high schools for three-plus decades. Indeed, the various ways in which his public-school teaching years have influenced his poetry style do much to justify the title of this book, *WORKS*.

If one is going to write poems for the real world, those poems better be interesting! That is especially true in our era in which cable TV, Facebook, Twitter, and Instagram have shortened people's attention spans and have often made it more difficult for traditional forms of literature to find an audience. Danny's smart and heartfelt poems are as attention-grabbing as any that contemporary readers will find. In his work, conversational language is infused with a cut-to-the-core intelligence, perceptive local imagery, refreshing humor, unique personal philosophies, and surprise phrasings: "New Jersey is not a place but / a state of mind" ("Winter Clouds in Hoboken"); "Seagulls peck French fries / off a white Mercedes Benz / on Washington Street" ("Winter Clouds in Hoboken"); "You can't fool a Shot / more than twice" ("Shot Family Values").

Danny's work highlights the joys of human life, while also tearing away sheets of denial to confront modern political and social hypocrisy: "On some levels / I consider myself the luckiest man alive. / I love my wife Caroline and / children Casey and Levi dearly" ("Last Man Standing"); "Thin-lipped men / of gun and missile carve our language / to make death and greed palatable / to our corporate-washed consciousness" ("Letter to Eliot"); and "In what phony religion shall we raise / our child?" ("Me and My Ego"). Some of Danny's poems offer poignant testimonies to the unavoidability of personal and family struggles—in his case, these struggles include being raised by a German Jewish mother who had tragically lost her eldest son and parents in Auschwitz before finding her way to the U.S., and growing up as a child with a mentally ill older sister who could sometimes scare her younger brother, and his other sister, with violent outbursts and attacks. After noting the losses his mother experienced in the Holocaust, Danny observes: "a person doesn't have to die to become a part of you, / but death fixes their presence within you" ("MOM"). Regarding childhood experiences with his often-institutionalized older sister, Danny recalls with his insistent personal honesty: "She repeatedly hit me / or bit me or pulled my hair. / When I cried, I got a lecture / about the mentally ill." ("Mental").

Anyone even slightly familiar with the songs of the Garden State knows that many New Jerseyans are "born to run" (Bruce Springsteen), born to seek adventure—whether from Bruce's hometown of Freehold or Danny's childhood home of Dumont—and that cars frequently play an essential role in the lives of those thrill-seeking young people in this highway-filled geography. In Danny's brilliant opening piece, "How to Write the Great Jersey Poem," he notes that young Jersey curiosity-seekers "Journey through ravenous tunnels / with the promise of . . . / adventure in the night," and they often search for those adventures in "a fast car / with a broken muffler." And in one of the book's funniest poems, "CARS," Danny provides readers with a history of the eccentric jalopies he has personally driven through North Jersey roads, including one which would only drive backwards and "which I nevertheless drove only / in reverse through the streets of my hometown."

Some of Danny's poems explore his high-school teaching years, looking at both the ways he hopes that he has inspired his students and the ways he knows that his students have inspired him: "Katrina is a gifted writer. Milagros works hard / and volunteers for everything" ("Morir Soñando"). Other poems focus on the problems and potential of his long-time and current mile-square hometown of Hoboken, New Jersey, just across the Hudson River from New York City. In "Give Us Back Our Town (Motherfucker)," Danny demands: "Give us back our town / consumed by developers, / politicians, realtors," and notes that the gentrifying city has lost some of its previous literary culture while participating in the all-too-common national trend of allowing private and charter schools to bring back, more than a half-century after the Supreme Court's landmark *Brown v. Board of Education* decision, a new form of racial segregation in schools: "you took the bookstores / and replaced them with nail salons," and "you opened charter schools / that separate the colors of our city."

In Danny's poetry, social evolution is incisively seen as an unfinished project. While he fears "human capacity for cruelty," he can also find a nugget of "beauty in most anything" ("Last Man Standing"). In a poem dedicated to his two sons, Casey and Levi, Danny sums up his view of a still-developing humanity: "We are not fixed   we are not whole / we are simple broken beings / needing time to restore." ("September Song").

One of the volume's most powerful poems is its closing one, "Invitation to Walt"—a piece calling for political bravery, honesty, and imagination—written for and during the hopeful (for progressives) protest days of Occupy Wall Street. In this piece, Danny asks America's first great democratic poet, Walt Whitman, to help us "not see America through rose-colored / blinders, but as it is, an unfinished kaleidoscope / cacophony created by imperfect human hands." He observes the need for the U.S. to recognize the international human rights to education and health care and writes, as a person with a long history of doing rewarding but difficult labor: "we need to restore the dignity of work / as well as the dignity of leisure from work." Ultimately, he asks Walt Whitman to "give me the courage to not be scared . . . to tell the truth." And he declaims, "It's time for us to dream big again," to "protect our glorious habitat," and to "Imagine America based on empathy and equality"—ultimately announcing "we're here, citizen poets for change."

With America having recently veered dangerously off course with the election (through an antiquated Electoral College system) of a dishonest, anti-union, anti-environmentalist, far-right narcissistic president, creating a new and better way forward will certainly require artists and activists to look and speak honestly, and to dream big. During the process of working as "citizen poets for change"—whether on a personal level, like working as a teacher, or on a broader activist level, like Occupy Wall Street—Danny reminds readers not to forget the need to take at least some time to celebrate the joys of life: "Champagne is destined to be drunk / not admired from a distance. / My advice dear reader: / Lift your glass, Drink up!" ("Champagne").

Some of the poems in this book will taste bitter. Some will taste sweet. And some bittersweet. But the eclectic mix of tastes in this unforgettable volume will always seem engaging and honest, and the poems inside will provide psychic nutrition and fuel to help readers get from one end of New Jersey—or whatever state of mind one chooses to live in—to the other. Here is a book to drink up.

—Eliot Katz, January 2017

How to Write the Great Jersey Poem

Start in the meadowlands
or the Turnpike
or on the Turnpike driving
through the meadowlands

in a car, a fast car
with a broken muffler
and faulty air conditioner.

Wind up down the shore
after sundown
listening to a bar band
drinking beer in a plastic cup.

Have a secret rendezvous
with a beautiful girl
or boy (your choice)
"Born to Run" plays in the background
or "Sandy" or "My Way" . . .
anything but "New York, New York."

Working-class roots
must be explored in depth:
Factory work, waitressing
while attending state college,
convenience store clerkery,
and drunken poetry readings
in extraterrestrial bars—
topics worthy of consideration.

Wax poetic over holiday celebrations,
Fourth of July fireworks,
suburban Xmas light displays,
Thanksgiving homecoming games,

blaring salsa street festivals
Memorial parades with hobbled
veterans and firetrucks,
inebriated St. Patrick's bar crawls
feasts for saints, brass bands snaking
through streets with statues
carried on ancient Italian shoulders.

Go sparingly on the adjectives
and adverbs, the grammar
of New Jersey is built
on nouns and verbs.
Description unbecoming.

Scatter the ashes of a loved one
in the Hudson
the Delaware
the Atlantic Ocean
according to temperament.

Occasionally, write about family,
the family you grew up with
or the family you raised:
A daughter talking to a god
beheld in empty hands,
a malingering son
slapped on the cheek,
the tears that follow,
your Dad the Jersey City cop
who dragged you off the shadowy
streets and thereby saved your life.

Journey though ravenous tunnels
with the promise of strange music,
glamour, adventure in the night.

Rail against, but accept corruption
for what it is—employment
opportunity for the village idiots
of your town and county.

Keep open relationships with
our friends from the South (Jersey),
an exotic people
whose antic descriptions
of devils, piney woods,
crosses burning in moonlit fields,
Atlantic City hijinks provide
fodder for many a homey tale.

Mourn the suicides and overdoses
of friends and lovers
who ventured to the City
with oversized dreams.
Record your melancholy
as the casket rests in the
ripped green grass.

Admire the gleaming Gotham
skyline from a distance.
Remember, it was erected for us.

Let the unknown unfold organically.
No matter what Camus says
New Jersey *is* the birthplace of existentialism.
Who can argue with a pair of longhaired
boys smoking Winstons
in front of 7-Eleven on a Saturday night?

Winter Clouds in Hoboken

are different than New York City clouds
occasionally cumulus, lately ominous,

biblical in fact. New Jersey is not a place but
a state of mind according to my Brooklyn students,

the last frontier between irrelevance and extinction.
Everything you think it is, and more.

New Jersey is whole lotta place(s). My place is Hoboken
where neighbors share home-brewed coffee

the morning after Sandy flooded basements
in apocalyptic power surge, then darkness.

Where brass bands carrying statues fire cannons
in honor of obscure Italian saints though the midday streets.

Graffitied walls proclaim PK Kid is alive, Viva!
Not art to be sold in galleries across the river.

Where an empty parking space is a conversation starter
and a drunk girl cries next to a smashed cell phone

on my stoop two weeks before Saint Patrick's Day,
a pool of green puddled at her feet.

Where we pretend we invented baseball
where everyone's grandma dated Sinatra.

Where the poets drink like poets
and are ignored like poets.

Where the ends justify the ends
and happy hours last all night.

Seagulls peck French fries
off a white Mercedes Benz
on Washington Street

The clouds are different
here. They just are.

9th Street Nocturne

No place more Jersey
than the 9th Street PATH station
in Manhattan at 2:30 Saturday morning.
Most New Yorkers don't know this place,
its entrance and exit a square hole
carved into an existing building.
Walking in from the street underground
to the train station is like walking through
a 3-D windswept H.R. Giger illustration,
hoses, wires, and dark rounded corners.

Let's be honest—everyone's drunk,
except those on drugs.
There are no bathrooms in the station.
Every few minutes a drunk will stagger
to the end of the platform and pee onto the tracks.
Nine out of ten times, it's a guy.
Occasionally, a uniformed Port Authority police officer
will pop out of a stainless-steel door at the end of the station,
grab the perpetrator and pull him back behind the door,
never to be seen again.
But this only happens once or twice a night.

There's not enough benches.
While over a hundred drunk and rowdy bridge
and tunnelers will be in the station at any time,
there's enough bench space for maybe twelve lucky souls.
The rest of us sit on the floor, propped up
against the tile columns in various states
of zombie consciousness. Every now and then
we are awakened from alcohol-induced slumber
by someone near us vomiting onto the tracks.

One train serves both Jersey City and Hoboken.

After midnight it runs every forty minutes.
Those with enough presence of mind
will get on the train going uptown,
take it to 34th Street and then take it back
downtown to New Jersey.
Spouses returning home moments
before sunrise have a built-in excuse.

Whether it be July or December,
the PATH station is usually a temperate 92 degrees,
the faint smell of sulfur adds to the ambiance.
It is not uncommon to see people shedding
articles of clothing as we play a virtual
slow motion game of strip poker.
The combination of heat, smell, time passing languorously,
and the alcohol (or drugs) coursing through our systems,
sometimes leads to temper flare-ups.
Something as simple as "why you staring at my girl?"
or as complex as "gimme another cigarette chief" triggers the row.
Usually some pushing and shoving, maybe a few punches thrown,
now and then a knife flashed, then the Port Authority cops
come out of the silver door at the end of the platform
and arrest the guilty parties.

About a year ago, one of the cops accidentally
discharged a tear-gas canister.
We all had to be treated outside.
We missed 2 or 3 trains.
When I got home at about 5 o'clock,
Caroline looked at me incredulously
as I told her my story.
I thought she had to believe me
because this time it was true,
but I could tell by her eyes she thought
I reached an unimaginative new low
in excuse-making.

Lunar Live

(at the Court Tavern in New Brunswick, New Jersey)

A couple of middle-aged men in polo shirts tucked in
over plump bellies stand up to the bar complaining
about the opening act of the Beach Boys concert
they are attending down the block at the State Theater.
Amazingly enough, I know the opening act
they are complaining about through one or two degrees
of separation but I keep my mouth shut because
I don't know if he's any good but I did root
for him on the tv show *Rock Star: Supernova*.

I call my buddy Robert Press in Pittsburgh:
"Guess where I am? . . . The Court Tavern,
but it's like an old man's bar now, and I think
I'm one of the old men."

Downstairs Lunar Ensemble is playing
and I love the word *ensemble* which I imagine
is French and adds a touch of elegance to a rock
band's name but I miss the word Bear
because Bear is part of the original band
and he's not here because his truck broke down.

Tonight they are joined by Martin Atkins
who is pounding the drums with a fury
that is both cleansing and life affirming.
Lunar's words flutter over the sonic throbs
and meanderings occasionally drowned out
by noise and feedback but it doesn't matter
because this is rock and roll or whatever
we call it and the drinks are cheap
so all is good and a guy in the band is playing

a theremin, which I've never seen in a band,
but I know is the sound at the beginning
of "Good Vibrations" which is a Beach Boys song.
And Sluggo's playing guitar and it sounds as hard
as it did a lifetime ago and the band and crowd is moving.

As Caroline and I watch the band I notice the crowd
a mixture of kids and people my age (dare I say older folks).
The women are wearing jeans and tank tops
and swaying in that New Jersey hippie chick sort of way.
The guys are long-haired and balding
and make no effort to hold in their guts while
others look rail thin intense and speed-ravaged
and all wear T-shirts and shorts
(after all it's summer) and drink beer from plastic cups
and I remember that these are my people
but I feel like a poser concerned
with style, appearance, and how I am seen.

Martin is still banging away on drums,
Sluggo's guitar is soaring over the theremin
and Lunar is standing next to me in the crowd
with a stoned smile on his face looking at the band
knowing how good they are and bobbing
his head rhythmically along with the crowd.

This is what my being needs,
a healing night of drink and music
at the Court Tavern in New Brunswick
where my New York pretensions
and concerns about aging are useless
impediments to my satisfaction
because I am alive
and the music is loud
and the beer is cheap

and the crowd is real
and my soul is clean
Lunar Bear Live
days into my 50th year.

CARS

New Yorkers will never understand
the power derived from driving
a new car home
in my case a new used car
this time a 2013 Hyundai Sonata
midnight blue whose speedometer climbs
to 160 miles per hour
an arousing number
perhaps beyond my reach.

Before this a green '98 Saturn
a utilitarian vehicle from
the last millennium
more plastic than metal
nevertheless a sturdy companion
who survived her share of bumps
and bruises navigating Hoboken's
surly stop and go streets.

Previously an '87 Chrysler LeBaron
a car with awful reviews
in *Consumer Reports*
that provided the smoothest ride
of my working-class life
until she got broadsided by a Mack truck
on a Harlem Street on the way to work.
Me thinking as the bulldog smashed into my side
"so this is what it's like to die,
hope it doesn't hurt too much,"
a crash I walked away from
unscathed in a state of shock.

Which was preceded by a 1982
Buick Regal nothing but trouble
that I should have been wary of
upon purchase from a fortune teller
in the Portuguese section of Newark
a natural lowrider without any modifications,
eventually stolen by wayward teens which
wound up being a windfall paying back
in insurance more than the car was
ever worth.

There was the 1980 AMC Eagle
station wagon with faux wood panels
which took Caroline and me cross-country
that had uncontrollable 4-wheel drive
which kicked into gear at the oddest times
and was constantly blowing tires on the
NJ Turnpike for no discernable reason.

Which followed a yellow '70 something
Datsun we named Roadkill
because it was in a constant state
of death throes and rattles
emitting a sulfurous stream of black smoke
every time it accelerated through a toll booth
rusted through its chassis yet refused to die.

There was the '67 Lincoln Continental
a tank disguised as an automobile
with suicide doors that comfortably
carried 8 inebriated teenagers to the
1975 Dumont High School Senior Prom
and once miraculously cruised from Amherst
to New Jersey on a half tank of gas
though it got about 6 miles a gallon.

And the '62 Studebaker that had a stone
instead of a carburetor that I used to deliver
Uncle Frank's Pizzas in high school until
it caught fire while driving on Madison Avenue
that the volunteer fire department
had to put out after only 3 months
of care and ownership.

Which was a replacement for my first
love, a white '66 Impala that I bought
for 40 dollars because it had been hit
by a garbage truck and was mangled
around the trunk but drove until the transmission
went a few months into my ownership
which I nevertheless drove only
in reverse through the streets
of my hometown oblivious to the cops
or the basic laws of physics.

Which I bought to ease the pain
of the loss of my '64 Rambler
with push-button transmission
which was never really mine but my Dad's
bought only a month before he died
and was totaled by my mother during
an ill-advised driving lesson
with my brother-in-law Leo
who was far from a great driver
and was promised to me in theory
when I came of age and which
I surreptitiously drove out the driveway
late nights after Mom was asleep
to pick up my buddies and the Diaz twins
in stoned teen fuck it all New Jersey abandon
that New Yorkers would never understand.

My Dad's many clunkers none more memorable
than the red '48 Chevy with the chrome hood ornament
a naked goddess with voluptuous mid-century
All-American breasts that Steve Martorelli and I would kiss
every morning on our way to school between
first and third grades for good luck
and because it was a thing to do
whom we named Minerva after the mermaid in *Diver Dan*
planting the seeds of unconditional love
between this man and my newest, my bluest
my darling set of wheels.

Give Us Back Our Town
(Motherfucker)

I made a phone call
to the future back in 1985 . . .

Today she answered
to show what we've become:

Future, now present, I'm not sure
I love you as much as the past.
We got what we wished for,
it's not a garden of delight.

Give us back our town
consumed by developers,
politicians, realtors and
youthful packs of clones.

You have taken it away
piece by piece
and I want it back.
You gave us yuppies with money
and bankers in training.
You won't go away, will you?

First you took the discount stores
and replaced them with realtors.
Then you raised the rents
and try and try to raise them again
then you raised the taxes
then you took the bookstores
and replaced them with nail salons
then you gave us Starbucks
and then you gave us more Starbucks.

And you opened charter schools
that separate the colors of our city,
though there's a King Day Concert
annually at the Episcopal church
so all can feel good about diversity
and how far Hudson County has come.
Just give us public schools that function
and programs for our teens.

You build parks on the outskirts of town
near the luxury enclaves of wealth
and trumpet it as a triumph of green,
as if green-space in Weehawken
benefits our community.

You revalue our homes
so old-timers pay more
and Wall Streeters pay less
and you call it equitable.

You took away our rock club
you let Maxwell's get away
our only sin was getting older
and raising children in this place
now we have artisanal pizza eight screens
tuned to ESPN, the soul of a flea.

Debt-inducing tolls through the tunnels
clogged PATH trains on the weekends
you give us never-ending bus lines
and throw up your hands in hasty defeat.

I'm talking to you, career politicos,
whatever you call yourselves;
be it reformers, Republicans,
bloggers, advisors, advocates
Hoboken Revolt, Kids First,

Move Forward
or Hudson County Democrats,
you sold us out again and again.

You give tax breaks to developers
but not the people who've been
in this town through the thin and thick.

But who can blame anyone
when the pie is for the taking
call it inevitability, progress, fate
Hoboken our home forever for sale.

Champagne

In my hands a green bottle
of Sunny Valley New York Champagne
given to my father (Siegfried) upon
his arrival in Hoboken from Germany
in 1928 which sort of matches
the 25.6 ounce bottle of Brut
aftershave I received after the death
of my brother-in-law's father (Paul) in 1992.
There's something satisfying
about collecting cheap green
American liquids of a bygone era.

May all your joys be pure joys,
and all your pain champagne.

I don't know much
about my father's early life in America
other than he was poor, very poor.
He sold gloves on the sidewalk in front of Macy's
during the Depression and would often walk back
the 100-plus blocks to his apartment in the Bronx
for years before he found factory work at Bendix
making airplane parts during WWII.

To life, to life, l'chaim!
L'chaim, l'chaim, to life!

The plan was to open the bottle on the birth
of his first child (my sister Carol) in 1944.
That didn't happen.
Then to open the bottle at the birth of his first son (me)
in 1957, but that didn't happen.
Then at Carol's wedding in 1964,
you get the picture.

My father died in 1972.
The bottle fell into my hands.
I was going to open it at my wedding,
then the birth of my first son (Casey) in 1988.
Didn't happen.
I threatened to open it to celebrate the Millennium.
Didn't.

May our sons have rich fathers and beautiful mothers!

Perhaps I'll open it at the birth
of my first grandchild. Maybe.
If not, it will fall upon Casey and Levi
to ceremoniously uncork it
upon my demise (whenever that will be)
though I hope they don't drink it
because it must be fermented beyond
romance, nostalgia, or reason.

May you never go to hell
But always be on your way.

Champagne is destined to be drunk
not admired from a distance.
My advice dear reader:
Lift your glass, Drink up!

Shot Family Values

(passed down through generations)

1. You can't fool a Shot
     more than twice.

2. Don't ask for much
     and you won't be disappointed.

3. May your children grow
     taller than you.

4. The Penis:
     If you don't use it, you lose it.

5. Avoid Germans, especially doctors,
     butchers, vegetarians, and teachers.

6. When push comes to shove
     move quickly.

7. Man maketh, and God taketh
     (or vice versa, I forget).

8. Be known for the product of your sweat
     not the sweetness of your perfume.

9. Wash your hands after a funeral.

10. Don't get your pussy where you
     get your paycheck
          (I once heard my father
          advise a young coworker).

11. Accept gifts without complaint.

12. Always remember:
    Everyone hates the Jews.
        Look where it got Jesus.

13. Take notes.

14. Two may keep a secret
    if one of 'em's dead.

15. Baseball is a metaphor for any aspect of life.
    He or she who says otherwise is uninformed.

16. Religion is the last refuge
    of the damned.

17. In the words of philosopher Red Auerbach:
    Think Yiddish, Dress British.

18. Listen with your eyes.

19. Never look into an open casket,
    especially if occupied.

20. Avoid the word *always*, always
    and *never* too.

21. Never forget . . .

The Grandeur of Willie

Uncle Willie
was the mascot
of Patton's Third Army.
Willie led the way
as they marched into liberated Europe
mounted high upon a snowy stallion
pressed into dress khakis
spit-shined riding boots
silver stirrups and spurs
sword pointing onward.

Patton's Army marched behind
Willie's hook nose
and five-foot frame
aiming towards glory
column after column
parading through the streets
of liberated France
and defeated nazi Burgs
for bloodshot German eyes
to see the swarthy face
of the conquering Jew.

Mental

"Daddy's coming . . . Daddy's coming . . . Daddy's coming . . ."
"No, Susan. Daddy's not here."
"Daddy's coming . . . Daddy's coming . . . Daddy's coming . . ."
"My God, Susan. Daddy's not coming. He's gone."
"Daddy's coming?"

Poor Mom. She's getting too old for this.
I'm getting too old for this.
Every other Sunday for twenty years
I drive Mom to Rockland Hospital.
I know the script by heart.

"Crinkies?"
"No, Susie, you already ate two packs of Twinkies."
"Crinkies?"
"I said no."
"Nilla pudding . . . nilla pudding . . . nilla pudding . . ."
"Yes, Susan, I have vanilla pudding for you at home."
"Pot roast?"
"Yes, Susan, Mommy made you a nice pot roast."
"Slice it?"
"Yes, I'll slice it when we get home.
Danny I'll make you a nice pot roast
sandwich when we get home."

God I wish they'd both be quiet.
Maybe the music will quiet Susie down.
Damn she's going to wear out the springs
with all that rocking. Uh-oh, red light
Better turn the music up.

"Green . . . green . . . make it green . . ."
"No, Susan, we have to wait for the light to change."
"Green . . . green . . . make it green . . ."

"Relax child, you must be patient."
"Green . . . one . . . two . . . THREEEEEEE!!!"

I hate this part.
Time to assert my authority
as driver and man of the family:
"Susie, shut the fuck up! Shut up!
Do I have to turn this car around
and take you back to the ward?"
"No."
"Do you understand?"
"Understand."
Now Mom looks hurt.
I wasn't yelling at her.
At least Susie's quiet.

My parents put Susie in a hospital
when I was born. For my protection.
When my Dad drove Susie home to Dumont
on Sundays, I would tell my friends
that she was my aunt from Germany
and rush her inside.

"Dumont Dumont here we come."
"That's right Susan over the railroad
tracks and we're home."
"Dumont Dumont here we come . . ."

Dad taught her that song.
He's been dead a long time.
He picked Susie up from the hospital
every Sunday for years.
That probably helped kill him.
I had to sit in the back seat
next to her. She repeatedly hit me
or bit me or pulled my hair.

When I cried, I got a lecture
about the mentally ill.
Crazy or not, she was ten years older
than me and it didn't seem fair.
Susie knows I'm bigger and stronger now
and that I wouldn't hesitate in hitting back.

"Licorice."
"No, Susan, no licorice."
"Nibs."
"No, Susan, not today. I don't have the money."
"Nibs . . . Nibs . . . Nibs . . . Nibs . . . Nibs . . . Nibs . . . Nibs . . ."
"Danny, do you think you could stop at the 7-Eleven
and get some Nibs? I need to get my cigarettes anyway."

A few months ago Susie hit me in the head
with a soda bottle as I was driving.
I calmly turned the car around
and drove back to the hospital.
Mom looked hurt,
as if I were punishing her.
Tough.

"Gotta take a shit."
"No, Susan, you wait until we're home."
"A shit."
"We'll be home soon."

If I could just wrap the left rear side
of this car around a telephone pole
it would look like an accident.
With my luck, I'd total the car
and Susie wouldn't even get hurt
and we'd be stuck in the street
waiting for a tow truck and she'd
be howling and everyone would

be staring and it would be awful.

I don't know how she manages to survive.
Once I saw her fall asleep in the bathtub
and slip under the water.
If Mom hadn't pulled her up
she would have drowned without
so much as a whimper.
She's going to outlive us all.
I just know it.

"Cheese. American cheese?"
"Yes, Susan, at home I have slices
of American cheese for you."
I hope she doesn't throw up
on the way back to the hospital.
She does sometimes.
I keep telling Mom not to feed
Susie so much sugar and meat,
But she doesn't listen.
At last . . . Forest Road.

"Susie, we're home."
"Chocolate pudding . . . chocolate pudding . . . chocolate pudding . . ."

My Bad Angel

doesn't always watch over me.
She puts things in my head.
She tells me things like:
"While having coffee this morning,
put your arms around the young pretty teacher
you are friendly with and pull her close to you . . .
kiss her passionately . . . you know she wants you . . .
look into her eyes . . . real men take what they want."
But I know better.
My bad angel loves me deeply.
She is my angel
but I don't trust her.

My bad angel is a beautiful
twenty-five-year-old woman
wearing too much lipstick,
a primitive woman dancing naked
in the moonlit forest of the mind
beheld by amber eyes.

My bad angel buys me drinks and
then has no money to pay for them.
She always lights my cigarettes.
She serenades my daydreams with Spanish
love songs of unrequited love.
She tells me to write poems when
I should be paying bills.
Her lips taste of bitter absinthe kisses
drunk in all-night underground cafés.
She suffers me with longing.

My bad angel comes to me at night and invades my dreams.
She takes the change from my pockets when I'm sleeping.

She took my leather jacket.
She wants me to shave my head.

My bad angel needled her way into angel-land
self-destructing and obstructing
my emotional merry-go-round.
My bad angel tried to strangle
my wife in her sleep.
She wants me all to herself.
We have a special relationship.
She tells me things she tells nobody else.
She tells me:
"Death is the truth of life.
Life is the air that we breathe,
the love that we keep,
the desire we touch,
the thoughts that we feel.
The body is a shell
that gives form to the living."

My bad angel tells me I'm a ladies' man
in spite of my face.
She makes me forget my anniversary.
She makes me buy presents for imaginary lovers.
She says it's okay to read my poetry to people
at trendy SoHo restaurants because I've already paid my dues.
My bad angel always reminds me to wear my grapevine suit
to dramatic happenings on Avenue B.
My bad angel makes me undress women in my mind.
She lets me look at dirty pictures.
She touches me yet can't be touched.
She would like to babysit my children
if I would let her.
She pushes me into the middle of fights at school.
She wants me to buy a gun.

She helped me assemble my switchblade.
She doesn't give a damn about my history.
She never ever listens to me.

My bad angel keeps other angels away from me.
She hardens me with desire for bodies
that are out of reach.
She has followed me from New York to Hoboken.
She is here right now.
She lives within me.
She doesn't need wings to fly.
My bad angel plays outside of time.
My bad angel took her own life
and still blames it on me.

She shows me glimpses:
The body a shell
that gives form to the living.
The living interconnected
to all the living that ever were.
Time, a road built upon shadows
of souls of all ever alive.
Time measures life,
God measures death.
God the Word . . .
Lovers embrace the edge of eternity,
naked forever after . . .
Smile, angel, smile,
your secrets are mine.

MOM

These are the last days.
Today my sister and I decided
we would put two morphine pain patches
on Mom, one on each shoulder.
The cancer has been eating away
at her body day after day.
She is slipping away
and there is nothing we can do
to slow the process of dying.
As her body shrinks and shrivels
her stomach grows distended
as the tumor grows.

My sister Carol is here
every day before work,
after work, often deep into the night.
If I were a Christian I'd call her a saint.
Thank God I'm not alone,
because nobody understands you
like a brother or sister can.
Carol feels guilty that we're not doing enough
for Mom. I feel we're doing what we can.

I am intrigued by the pain patches.
They are filled with morphine
which is released over time.
What would happen if I put one on?
How would it feel?
I ask Carol if she feels like trying
a pain patch and she looks at me
as if I'm out of my mind.

But Mom is the one who is dying right now
in front of us and there really isn't a damn thing
we can do about it. She's doing it, dying that is,
with dignity; perhaps more than she usually has in life.
She doesn't ask for much, doesn't complain,
and doesn't want to trouble us with talk of her fate.
She's often in la-la land because of the patch,
slipping in and out of consciousness.

A couple of days ago she smelled a piece of soap
that Jessica my niece (her granddaughter)
had given her and responded
"this is the perfumed decadence
of sprightly virgins awaiting defilement."
Jessica and I looked at each other. We asked her
to explain herself, but Mom was done talking.

Six weeks ago Mom was okay.
She was just plain old Mom.
Then she started having dizzy spells
and the doctor came to the conclusion
that her diabetes was out of control.
Unfortunately, the doctors discovered
lung and liver cancer.
Mom has only been out of the hospital
to come home to die.

My mom doesn't like to face her fate.
She doesn't admit she has cancer,
at least by name.
She calls it "the little cherry in my lung."
She thinks now that she's given up smoking
it'll all go away.
I guess she doesn't really think that.

A few hours ago, while I was giving her some water,
she stopped drinking, opened her eyes wide
and said "you will always be my sweetheart,
because you're such a gallant nazi fighter."
I asked her if she knew who I was and she said
"of course, you are my little boy Danny,
my brave little boy."

I'm the baby of the family.
Mom had four of us really.
Her firstborn, Ernst was killed
by the nazis at Auschwitz
along with Mom's parents.
Ernst died at six years old,
so the two of us never lived
on this earth at the same time,
but his presence is felt.
Then there's Susan
who is three years younger than Carol.
Susan is autistic, retarded, schizophrenic
and probably three or four other diagnoses
that haven't been given names yet.
She's been in mental hospitals
since the day that I was born.
When Mom dies, Carol and I
will take over the responsibility
of looking in on Susan for the rest of our lives.
Again, thank God there are two of us.

The doctor told me in advance
that Mom was too old and her cancer
too far gone for chemo to do anything
but cause more suffering.
After examining my mom, who was not strong
enough to unbutton her blouse,

the doctor took me out of the room,
closed the door halfway and said
in a very loud voice: "If it were my mother
I would suggest hospice care.
It's not like you think.
The patient can control their lives
and end their lives with dignity."
Of course he said it in a loud enough
voice so Mom could hear.
Mom made the decision later that afternoon.

Hospice care is not like you think.
Mom has a fulltime live-in caregiver
named Beryl who is from the Bronx
who has become very important to all our lives.
Beryl is as strong as Carol and I put together,
and fortunately is sweet and seemingly has a lot
in common with Mom. They hit it off,
maybe because they're both immigrants,
maybe because they've both experienced
heartbreak in regards to their children.
One of Beryl's sons was gunned down
right in front of their house.
But Beryl, thank God, is healthy,
and Beryl is here, and Beryl keeps Mom company,
and Beryl tries to make Mom eat,
and Beryl listens to Gospel
music on some all-Gospel station I didn't know existed,
and our lives revolve around Beryl.
I'll say it again and again: Thank God for Beryl.
Hospice care means that Mom will die
in her own room in her own house
with her children nearby.

Dealing with a death is not as bad as everyone thinks.
You're sad, but it's not an overwhelming, debilitating grief.
It's more like a piece of you is pulled out leaving a hole.
With time the hole slowly fills in and the dead person's spirit,
or essence, or whatever, becomes a part of who you are.
I guess a person doesn't have to die to become a part of you,
but death fixes their presence within you.
It gives form to a shadow. I believe.
If Mom makes it through the night I'll be surprised.
I think I'll take off work tomorrow.
I should be around when the time comes.

A miracle at this point in time would be downright cruel.
I don't go to work in the morning.
A middle-aged man probably has no right
to feel like an orphan,
but we're not talking about rights here,
are we?

The light of dawn shadows
the walls of Mom's bedroom
as morning darkness
becomes day.
The clock on the kitchen
wall doesn't stop ticking.
It keeps right on moving . . .

Susie

My sister Susan is fifty-one years old
and lives with a black family
in Poughkeepsie, New York.
This family adopted her,
(they're getting paid to care for her of course)
and truth be told Susan is getting better care today
than at any time in her life.

Carol and I don't really know how to relate
to Susan because we see the very bad schizophrenic girl
who terrorized our childhoods with screaming fits, hair-pulling,
biting, and unidentified flying objects.
Of course she is a mentally retarded autistic woman
who people see as sweet and innocent.

For some reason I show my friend Jack Wiler
the anecdotal psychiatric history of Susan that has been sent to me
by the newest in a long line of social workers
which includes statements such as:
"The mother was described as sensitive,
overprotective and depressed . . .
The father appeared to be submissive
and also overprotective on initial interviews . . .
There is a strong history of mental illness in both families . . .
During testing, Susan's behaviors were noted to be bizarre;
she engaged in rocking, tearing paper, jumping,
spontaneous whirling, facial grimacing, inappropriate smiling
and looking over her shoulder in a fearful manner . . .
She sat for hours sucking her thumb while wetting her pants . . .
Susan spent most of her time rocking and talking to herself . . .
She was autistic and appeared to be in a world of her own . . ."

And then the phone rings.
And when I come back Jack is crying.
Now I hate it when men cry in front of me,
but I really hate it when men cry about
how fucked-up my life is.
Jack explains how it just seems as if Susan is not all that crazy
and it was my parents who were somewhat crazy
and didn't know how to deal with Susan's behavior.
I become defensive and explain to Jack
that while my mom and dad did not fit
the stereotype "American Dream" family they did their best
and did what they could.

At this point Jack is so far away from where I'm at
that I realize he couldn't possibly comprehend
the difficulties facing a poor immigrant family,
particularly my immigrant family.
So I stop talking.

Having read many psych reports over my life,
I know that they have a tendency of making
everyone involved with the insane seem insane themselves.
Then, still wiping the tears from his eyes
Jack tells me that he understands why I never clean up
around the house, and that every woman he's ever known
would not put up with my sloppy behavior.
But now he understands why my wife Caroline accepts
my behavior, and he knows when I say I don't see or care
about the mess surrounding me I really must be telling the truth.

I pour Jack another drink.
And I begin to think it is Jack who is insane.
He's the one who irons his T-shirts.
He's still wiping away tears and I feel guilty
for not having the depth of character
Jack has projected upon me.

I don't like doing housework because I'm deeply lazy.
It's not my mother's fault.
But I don't tell Jack today because
I don't want to disappoint him.

The mother in Susan's new family is named Hawa
and she is about seven years younger than me
and she takes Susan to the mall, and to church,
has painted Susan's fingernails bright red,
and her friends accept Susan as part of the family.

When outsiders see Susan they don't see
the monster that Carol and I see.
I once showed my wife pictures of Susan
expecting her to recoil in horror.
Caroline betrayed no emotion.
"Doesn't she look insane? Look at her.
That's how a mentally ill person looks," I coaxed.
"I guess," was all my wife said shrugging her shoulders.
She didn't see what I saw.

Caroline and my boys have never met Susan,
though I regale them with amusing anecdotes about
strange things Susan has done, like plastering
American cheese slices on her breasts as she took a bath
or screaming in such a high-pitched decibel level and tone
after a cop pulled me over for going through a red light
that he bumped his head on my car and let me go
without a ticket.

I don't tell them about how Susan once pulled my hair
with such force I thought it would tear right off
my scalp, or how when she was in school
she painted the walls of the bathroom with shit
and my mother was called in to clean it up,
or how she caused Mom to have a nervous breakdown

by almost throwing me out the window
or how she made the first thirteen years
of Carol's life a total nightmare in
her role as the little sister from hell.

Carol and I drive to Poughkeepsie
to visit Susan.
She smiles rocking back and forth,
before she starts crying "I want my Mommy,
I want my Mommy, MomMomMommy."
Carol and I reassure Susan
that we too miss Mom
but she's not here
but we are here
and we always
will come to visit our Susie
because she is our sister.

Allyson,

I felt bad today for telling you
that Kanye's "Bound 2"
was the worst song I ever heard.

You said you really liked it
and said no more than that,
though I know you were annoyed.

I went home and listened
to it again and again and
again.

Three times.
I didn't watch the video.
I just listened.

I still don't love it.
But I don't hate it either.

I realized being young,
or not too old means
listening with fresh ears,

being able to hear the beauty
or truth that someone else
can hear.

Somehow, I forgot that.
Thanks for the reminder.

Danny

Morir Soñando

(with a dash of rum)

Been doing this for 22 years.
You should know better, but you don't.
The principal who hired you as assistant principal
without a license is an unmitigated bitch
and on your case because you are sympathetic
to the new teachers. She hired you
the people person, to improve morale
which you have done by taking the staff
out for drinks on Friday afternoons.
Now she hates you for it.

Relegated to cafeteria duty 3 periods a day.
Every day.
The job: keep the thuggish boys
from the high school slated to close
off the fresh-faced girls from your school.
Your life sucks.

But, there's Isabel, Katrina, Milagros, and Neli
period seven for Honors Spanish II
which you teach though your knowledge
of the language doesn't extend beyond
"¿Dónde está la biblioteca?"
You do this because the regular teacher,
an Orthodox Jew from Mexico City
spends every afternoon in your office
crying bitterly, asking Why? Why? Why?
She does not have a way with kids.
You do the honorable thing
and take her four most fluent students
and teach them Spanish.

They read García Márquez, Lorca, and Julia Alvarez
in Español while you teach in English,
then they work together in Spanish
and write essays which you give to
the nervous Spanish teacher to grade.

Katrina and Milagros are in your English class,
Katrina is a gifted writer. Milagros works hard
and volunteers for everything,
handing out papers, reading aloud,
erasing the board, translating phone calls.

Sometimes you wonder if Isabel's jeans are painted on,
why she smells like lavender and mango at the same time.
She confides that she has not seen her father
in ten years. He has another family in DR.
It's flattering that she chooses to sit next to you
on the bus trip to Boston, falling asleep with her head
on your shoulder through Connecticut
and wonder why and what for she wants you so badly
to meet her mother who she is sure you will like.

One day Katrina brings in coquitos,
Puerto Rican eggnog.
You all agree it's delicious.
Then she tells you it's spiked with rum
and you worry you're going to lose your job.
She tells you she was only kidding,
but you're not so sure.

Milagros teaches you Puerto Rican songs about ole San Juan.
Everyone sings along. The next day she brings in Shakira
and Calle 13 and the girls dance, hips shaking
and jiggling while mouthing the words
and you know this is wrong,
even though Isabel says ¿Maestro, cómo se supone
que cantamos sin mover nuestros cuerpos?

Maybe it's a cultural thing
though *you* can sing without moving your entire body.

Neli, the anorexic, comes in drunk one day
and throws up all over her Math class.
You offer her a Life Saver and she looks
at you like you're crazy, or worse, an old man,
"Do you know how many calories that has?"
As assistant principal, you call her parents
and send her to counseling.

The next day she comes to class with
a handwritten note (full of hearts over the i's)
thanking you for caring, and telling you she's
not mad that you called her parents,
and it's obvious you care about her well-being
more than her parents ever will.
The note says she's thankful to have you.
You wonder if this is at all appropriate
full well knowing the answer
but what are you going to do?

Milagros arrives late for class
in tears "A man touched me on the subway.
Why do they always pick on me?
What is it about me, why me?"
You console her and tell her it's not her,
there are a lot of creeps out there
especially on the trains. You tell
her to be aware, which is the best
you can offer as she sobs uncontrollably
as Isabel whispers something in Spanish.

For the final exam the girls prepare
a feast for the other Spanish class
morir soñando (orange drink and milk)
which is hopefully not spiked,
plates of arroz con habichuela,

empanadas, tostones, pernil,
dulce de leche, and mango ices.

They wear slinky shiny dresses, blue eye
shadow and fire red lipstick for the fiesta.
They dance to "Livin' la Vida Loca," again wiggling
and jiggling and you worry what
the nervous Spanish teacher will think.
What will happen if the principal walks in.
The other students lose all sense of decorum,
make a conga line snaking around the room
before sitting down to the feast.

The girls each earn grades of 95 for Honors Spanish II
except for Neli, who was absent a few times too many
so she gets a 90. The year ends.
You leave the school,
get a job in a dismal school
where the students wear uniforms.
The year grinds to a close.

You go to graduation in Williamsburg
4 bouquets of tulips in hand.
The principal tries to have you removed.
"Have you no shame?" she shrieks.
You wave her off like a bad dream.
Katrina goes to a near Ivy college in Boston,
Milagros attends a Catholic university in Virginia,
Ysabel moves back to Santa Domingo
to live with her abuelo,
Neli gets a job at Macy's doing makeup
on the first floor.

Facebook erases time and distance.
Isabel, Katrina, Milagros, and Neli
Lolitas, luces de tu vida
lights of your life.

Notes on a Train Between Bayonne and Hoboken

Beware means Be aware
Be aware of non-Asian friends
who make you take off your shoes
when you walk through the door.
Chances are you will smoke some pot
but they control the music
and the conversation
and will steal your lighter
which you will be powerless to retrieve.

Be aware of the phrase "just sayin'."
It usually follows an offensive statement.
Same holds true, in reverse
for "I'm not a racist, but . . ."

Be aware of politicians
who call themselves reformers.
They likely wish to privatize
public institutions you depend on.
When they're out of office
rest assured they will profit mightily.

Be aware of pop singers
who rely on autotune,
they will lip-sync their way
through the course of your life.

Be aware of charismatic speakers
who overuse the pronoun "they."
They will turn on you
the moment you disagree.

Be aware of the woman or man
who repeatedly asks, "How are you feeling?"
Chances are they will tell you
how they're feeling over and over again.
The upkeep will be expensive.

Be aware of reality tv
stretching the boundaries
of acceptable narcissism.
You will feel better about yourself
but worse about humanity.

Be aware of Christian anxiety
during the holidays,
of shopping malls on Black Friday
of Xmas wish lists,
of those who speak for Jesus.

Be aware of Amazon drones,
a technological new world order,
harbinger of things to come,
Maybe it is time to get a gun.

Be aware of poets
whose gift for theory
exceeds their talent
with language.
They will be canonized
after you have been forgotten.
They will read their work at St. Mark's
while you're on Avenue B.

4,000 Jews Can't Be Wrong

(or Scribblings on a Napkin Alone in a Bar)

"Who told 4,000 Israeli workers at the Twin Towers
to stay home that day?"

Thus spoke Baraka
poet laureate of the Garden State
having found these facts on the Internet
and sure enough it's there.

I found his facts on some neo-nazi
and English-language Arab websites
but nobody said anything about Israelis
though the sites did mention the 3 or 4,000
Jews who allegedly stayed home on 11 September 2001.

Which makes me wonder why nobody told
Peter Feidelberg, the young Hoboken Jew
who died with his fiancée Meredith Ewart
in the Twin Towering Infernos
whose short life was awkwardly marked
by my youngest son's hand as a star
on an oversized canvas American flag
made by children that hangs in city hall
each star a Hoboken life lost.
I guess they were out of the Zionist loop.

I imagine other Jews must have died on 9/11.
For that matter, nobody called to warn me
but I'm not big enough on the Jew chain
to warrant a suicide terror alert call.

I didn't know that the Twin Towers had 4,000 Israeli workers,
they probably must have been undercover Israeli spies.
Thank you, Amiri, for opening my eyes.

A poet friend who happens to be
a Jew told me he considered Baraka
a modern-day Ezra Pound,
a poet of talent and charisma
who stubbornly holds onto crackpot
ideas with the Jew at the apex of
his paranoia. I wanted to disagree.

I guess the lines 17 stanzas above,
"Who knew why Five Israelis was filming the explosion
And cracking they sides at the notion"
is not so offensive because it must be true.

Amiri, I have prized my connection to you
from the first time we met:
young Rutgers poets Eliot Katz and I
brought a big bottle of wine
to dinner and Cheryl Clarke scolded
us for bringing alcohol to the table
of a famous Black Muslim, you smiled
and said "Thank God someone
brought something to drink."
I usually admire your fight,
relate to your height, same as mine
relish Amina's hugs and drunken toasts,
and joy of life, your New Jersey soul,
Newark home, your words that spit
as they sing . . .
But you're wrong
on this thing,
Amiri, you are wrong.

I don't believe in a poet laureate
or a hierarchy of poets set up
by any government or arts institution
any more than I believe the manufactured

emotional competition of the slam
brings out the best in poets or
that random ramblings of language
poetry brings revolutionary change
to the way we see or be or
that self-inflicted bondage
and discipline of formalistic verse
offers insight towards our humanity,
then again I am a throwback
to a simpler day
and I simply refuse to hate . . .

I am feeling squeezed from the left
of course squeezed from the right
like an empty toothpaste tube
my politics squeezed into "being a Jew"
doesn't matter what I might think
about abortion or Enron or the ethics of oil
who ever knew
it had to come down to this?
I should have known to know.

Then again, why should I care?
I am a wound
I am a scar
blue tattoo
and yellow star
I'm on a first name basis with God
I never really knew for sure
that we're the source of mankind's woe
the pure historical ebb and flow
bloodlust sharpened tooth of wolf
our elimination might be the cure
of the world's ills and the gulf
between the rich and poor
and racism and antisemitism too.

Who ever knew
I didn't know
I should have known
Who knew?
Did you?

The Blame Game

Who me? you? who? me?
who's to blame?
Who's at fault?
Who stole the teeth
from Betty Lou's smile?
Blame the poor
It's not my fault
Blame the Blacks
I didn't do it
Blame the Jews
killers of our favorite savior
Blame se habla Spanglish
Blame book readers
women with hairy legs
Blame nose rings
Hostess Twinkies
Japanese baseball
welfare mothers
and baggy pants.
Blame the 60s
the Kennedys
union workers
who dare to ask
for more.
Pin the blame
on the donkey.
Blame Oliver Stone
for Nixon.
Blame your watch
for being late
as you wait
behind the locked gate

for your voice
to arrive.
Blame teachers
and students
and girls
in tight pants.
Blame them all
for the fall
of American skies.
Blame Israel for 9/11
Obama for fascism
Atheists for terrorism
Name the blame
Hillary and roll
her in dirt.
Everybody now
play the blame game
blame them
not me.

IV

Letter to Eliot

Dear Eliot, Why can't I be more like you?
I get sad when I think too much.
I know you are not that way and I envy you.
Just when I'm about to grasp some obscure concept
like how long us commoners will continue
to lie back and let the monied have their way,
an old lover comes down to distract me.
She is naked, radiant, haloed.
"Stay dead!" I yell to my guardian angel,
"if you're not going to help me."

The empty days of summer torture me
with hopelessness spread like a coarse blanket
atop my solipsistic existence. Thin-lipped men
of gun and missile carve our language
to make death and greed palatable
to our corporate-washed consciousness
to ready our weary acceptance of "the ways of the world"
and I fail to resist because I've heard it all
so many times before it begins to take hold.

At the gym I listen to a Buzzcocks song over and over again
"Life's an illusion, Love is a dream.
Life's an illusion, Love is a dream."
And I wonder why couldn't it be a more glorious dream
and what exactly will the logistics of the afterlife be?
I need to redirect my focus on the moments fleeting by
and success has proven more elusive than imagined,
the shine of youth wore off decades ago.

Outside, three drunk Hoboken girls are falling
over the garbage cans, sprawling hair, belly flesh,
a lone flip-flop on the unforgiving sidewalk,

a bad beer commercial come to life in front of my window.
One is accusing her friend of making a play for her guy.
The air is wet with humidity and feminine angst
as I try to plot a course for my days to follow,
distracted by the sadness and the madness of the real
and my flawed smoldering dreams.

But El, maybe I do all right for a dreamer
truth be told I've had a ball
though I'm a tangle of insecurities
and aim too much to please.

Progress Report—October 2010

—for Jack Wiler

Life doesn't wait for the dead.
I know you'd want it that way
but I'm not so sure,
'cause now I'm a year older
and things do change.

America's turned right and the optimism we shared
last year has been stolen by the ugly folks
and Jack, I don't know how to say this but, white people
have gone crazy and it's really scary,
I need someone to laugh with
at the stupid shit people profess to believe.

You know how we used to sing
"Nobody ever died for dear old Rutgers"?
Well, that ain't exactly true of late:
A freshman killed himself from shame,
or bullying, or insanity, or circumstance,
but it's a tragedy still the same
and if you run into Tyler Clemente,
guide him through the afterlife,
try to show him a good time.

You have left your place
on the ascending Jacob's ladder
of American poets but no one
has taken up your rung,
willing to wrestle with angels
and demons simultaneously.

Bedbugs have invaded Manhattan
and you're not here to stem the tide

to offer sage advice and wisdom
to the itching masses
desperate for pest control salvation.

Jack, I hate to admit I've somewhat
lost track of Johanna, but if I remember
correctly, there were days when
you wondered where she was hiding
and when she was coming back.

Your brand new book *Divina Is Divina*
was on sale at the Dodge Poetry Festival.
I stood next to two gorgeous young women
who had copies in their hands, and I almost
volunteered to sign them but I figured
that might be inappropriate somehow, so
I played it cool, though the thought was there.

This past year we had a funeral
in your beloved Wenonah
put together by Mick and Ted,
a Dodge reading somewhere in Jersey,
a memorial service at Le Poisson Rouge
where we got wildly drunk and sentimental.
In the late spring we scattered your dust
in the Hudson off the Hoboken pier.
Teresa and John scattered the remaining
ashes at the Frost Place in August.

It's October 20, 365 days since you
left this mortal coil, the day
my father died in 1972 (3 lifetimes ago)
and my grades are due tomorrow
and life goes on, except when it doesn't
and your book is on my kitchen table
but you're not here.

Now it's November and we're having one more party
for you and your book
Divina Is Divina and its striking cover
and you're with us in spirit
and you're with us on paper
and on these bleeding pages
where you still say the things
we're not supposed to say
and the world is still spinning off its axis
and the bills still pile up at home
and we're all broke
and if this lame-brained nation of salesmen
with nothing left to sell is my life
or anyone else's we're all fucked.
So let's have another glass of wine
for the poets among us, within us,
above us, living and dead
whose visions connect us
with the eternal swirl beyond . . .

Mo's Bar April, Fort Greene

Vaginas and Crucifixes and Blood
says Tim, that's what I want in a poem
big V, big C, big B.
Nobody can disagree as we stand
on the corner of DeKalb and South Portland
sucking on cigarettes weighing the implications . . .

and so begins the weekend.
Miguel Algarín inside the bar, drunk
ready to have a serious conversation
about the trouble with Nancy.
A.J. the waitress knows what
I want to drink before I do.
Stephanie's tattoos give my eyes
a necessary drunken focal point.

Robin tells us of Elizabeth Bishop
and Lota in Brazil, of infidelity
and suicide and moving on.
Adam speaks of a Sea World
water slide past dolphins
at 60 miles an hour.

Never-ending winter over,
today's the day where everything
pops and Brooklyn's blooming
green, bud-luscious.

Welcome to the spring
Mr. Pollyanna. *L'chaim!*
Have another drink.

Earlier today Emilie showed me
a book about reading eyes,

said it reminds her of when I stop
walking, deep in thought,
it provides a key to what
might be in my mind

though I know the truth:
sometimes I just stop
to let the world spin
as I take it in and marvel
at the wonder of it all
like Mary Tyler Moore
on a sunny day.

Me and My Ego

have a problematic relationship.
By all rights she should be a man
but is a 19-year-old anorexic waif
with a poetic gift for self-destruction
who masquerades as a bosomy diva
       with a heart of gold.

Though she is fragile, she is my master,
gotten me hooked on the narcotic buzz
of praise and flattery.
And she's a cheap date who I like to get
fucked up, so I can have my way with her.

My ego is a trickster who sent me on a quest
with a thoughtful gift in hand
to soothe a burdened poet friend
who I was sure was sad because she read
my latest story and was touched by the immense
talent and sensitivity of my words,
when in fact her tears were caused
by a computer delivery problem
in her office that could best be
       resolved by FedEx, not me.

My ego has fallen for my alter ego
and all sorts of chaos has ensued:
In what phony religion shall we raise
our child? What striped shirt
shall I wear to work today? Who's the object
       of tonight's desire?

She consistently reminds me
that I am irresistible to females
and males of all shapes, sizes,

colors, and ages who want to know
and be close to me for my keen
intellect, weather-beaten face,
mysterious aura of unspoken pain,
energetic defense of shaky beliefs,
and deep commitment to looking
              as if I care.

My ego pushes me to pursue
women out of my league
and beyond my range of experience
who will find creatively
subtle ways to punish me.

She is a seeker of those that would
do her harm, put her down,
roast her in her own desires.
The more dangerous the game
the more attractive the hunt.

My ego comes off as a greedy bitch,
while in fact she's a needy bitch.
Those who don't know her well
think she's full of herself
when all she really wants is certain
chosen people to love her
              with all their might.

I sometimes wish she'd take a day
or a year off from leading me around.
Though I love her with all my heart
she never loves me quite enough.
I fear she'll leave me soon
for someone taller with a drier wit,
a muscular martial artist who'd
maim me for the sport of it.
Maybe she's already gone.

My ego is my vanity,
she doesn't miss a trick.
My ego is a nervous laugh
I need to have to win.
My ego is my missing piece,
I love to hear her sing.
Listen to her siren song
cascading through the wind.

At Baraka's House

for a party
in Newark
for Piri Thomas
thrown by my friend
Nancy Mercado.
Hilton Ruiz
jazz legend
playing tropical
plinkety plonk
waterfall melodies
of a distant island
on living room piano.

I sit on the floor
drinking my beer
talking to Steve Cannon
who is not drinking
anymore
for today
I try not to stare
up Pili's skirt
at her red
thong panties
what's beneath
inches from my eyes
as she turns and
leans over the piano.

My jeans
now stretched tight
as Pili's bottom
winks salutations.

I can't get up
to mingle
with literary icons
and revolutionaries
pole pointing north
dead-reckoning
to object of desire.

I sip my beer
and think of all
the major and minor poets
assembled here tonight,
my eyes focused
on the floor
thinking
immortality
revolution
immorality
revolution
baseball
poetry . . .

The Living Legend

put his dick
on the table
in the bar
on Avenue B.

I was shocked,
until I saw
what an unobtrusive
penis he owned.

Then I wanted
to put my dick
on the table,
to show him
how a true poet
was hung.

But my wife
wouldn't let me.

I drank another
beer, fighting
the urge to
plunk down
my shlong on
the wooden table.

I can see it,
everyone silent,
all eyes upon me,
the only sound
in the universe
my drunken pecker,
sloshing around in

a puddle of beer
on the table
in the bar
on Avenue B.

Thrown out on
my soon to be
immortal ass
into the wet
darkness
of
a
drunken
night.

My Money

It's my money
not yours
It's my money
I need more
my money
It's not enough
my money
I don't have to share
my money
I keep it close
my money
nobody's going to take it away
give it away
to loud crude people
with funny names
and bad habits.

It's my money
I've watched it grow
into big money
piled majestically high
to the feet of God
who has a taste
for the sweets of gelt.
It's all my money
glittering sensually
in midnight dreams
of forbidden favors
bought and sold.

It's my money
the New Deal is done gone
no more govment handouts

welfare cheats beware
socialized medicine . . .
I think not.
I buy paintings
to support the arts
Ha   Ha   Ha   (suckers!)

It's my money
fuck the poor
and their many children
let them get a job
let them pay for school
let them eat welfare cheese
make them go away
beat them down
into the ground.
It's my money and
I want it back.

It's my money
gonna buy me
favors and friendships
of painters and
poets and
models and
cardinals and
maybe even
you.

It's my money
my reason for being
my money
my business
my life
life is a business
everything for sale.

America: I love
this decorated hell
that feeds me opportunities
and hears my voice
above all others.

My money
don't give it away
to those who claim to be in need.
Nobody needs it
more than me
I need my money.
I need:

> a new BMW
> a vacation house
> liposuction
> hair replacement
> season tickets
> tax deductions
> fur for my mistress
> Ryan's ear
> an ambassadorship
> a magazine with my name
> on the cover
> Aspen, Colorado

My money
I spend it
as I wish.
My workers are grateful
that it is my money.
They show their appreciation
by washing my car
taking my suits to the cleaner
doing magic tricks for my children.
My employees,

they love me
because I'm tough but fair
fiscally responsible.

My money
not your money
don't touch it
Mom and Dad
worked hard for it.
My money
cultivated like an ancient orchard
bearing fruit for me and mine.
My money
don't stare at it
get to work
make me more
take your hungry eyes
out of my sight.
It's my money
I want more.

September Song

—for Casey and Levi

What flame   what smoke   what
       twisted steel   what
lifetimes pass in the blink of an eye
what blue sky opens toward ascension
Scent of burning metal rains
       ash like carbon snowflake hell
the images remain
       shudder and collapse
O my sons
Listen to my September Song.

Those who live for vengeance
       live for Death
Those who speak to us in the name of God
       speak of what comes after Death
Those who refuse to leave preconceived political
       disease behind bring rusty Death
Those who cannot shut up—cannot listen—
       cannot feel the gnawing trauma
       of a single quiet grieving man
       strangle spirit Cold.

We are not fixed   we are not whole
we are simple broken beings
needing time to restore
What chance change when
there are deals to be made
victims to blame
new hearts to break
elections to steal
lotteries to win
the new fall tv season to begin?

On what throne in what sky
            sits God above the mortal eye?
Why can we not ask what for and why
What the reason for the dragonfly?
Are we born to die alone?
Will we be safe in our bullseye home?
What means life but a universe within?
My voice mere whisper in the scheme of things.

I don't want to be told
            what to think anymore
I know what I saw with my eyes
I want to love
            but can't swallow the rage
I made these words
            they're all I have
fragments of ideas
            steely armor pierced
fragments of fears
            colossal monuments last
only so many years   how long
            flickers the burning ember
                of an extinguished Life?

What flame   what smoke   what
            twisted steel
what raw nerve exposed
            how long to heal?
O my sons
Listen to my song!

Last Man Standing

I.
I have yet to find my place in the world.
I have played the lonely bookworm in my home
towns Hoboken, New Brunswick, Dumont
and for that matter, San Francisco and New York
and I imagine the same would hold true in Paris,
Amsterdam, or Tel Aviv.
It has been glorious and lonely,
and those I've left behind
through distance, death, or disappointment
are deeply part of who I am.

By some measures my life
has been a profound failure
and to an objective observer
nothing is about to change real soon.
I have squandered my gift of words
keeping metaphors and images
locked in my mind
to eventually wither and die on the vine
letting moments and epochs pass by
with nary a mention
because buried memories
are razor-sharp painful
to dig up to the surface
of current happy smiley me
and I won't sacrifice my heart
for love or poetry anymore.

The phone doesn't ring like it used to
and I have turned gray smoking cigarettes
awaiting the call that puts me on the road
to rock star ego brimming immortality.

I have watched the best minds
of Allen Ginsberg's generation grow old and die
I have said my goodbyes.

An interior voice tells me
take vitamin E drink green tea
to wash my hands after I pee
listen closely before I speak
count to ten before I get mad
pluck the gray from my beard
read *Ulysses* ride my bike
make out a will lay off beer
avoid the mirror
record my dreams.

My soul has grown timid
like a shallow brook burbling
bucolicly in the backyard
of some millionaire's retreat:
Nowadays I go with the flow
floating from a leafless bough
that has scarred my spirit growth.

I personalize my parents' history
nazis nazis everywhere
I see nazis in your stare
smiling while profiling
goose-stepping and sieg-heiling
down strip mall America's boulevards
pistols smoking
hate and blood and fire
pollutes the air
as crowds of Joes and Josephines
look the other way.

My ghost brother is eternal
shadow, a boy touching me

to wake up from nighttime
graveyard slumber
forever being murdered
for being a Jew.
A boy who watches over
who lives my life inside of me
who sees what there is to see
of this newborn century
through his brother's eyes
who is forever six years old
leading me down unfolding
path that is my future as well as his.

Above all
I fear
human capacity for cruelty
little boys shoot little girls
for no reason possible at all
cops shoot unarmed black men
for being black and maybe poor
we bomb who we please
simply because we can
a gang of teenage boys throw stones
at a wounded hawk trembling
beneath a bush in the park
the strong beat up the weak
the rich eat up the poor
the blessed stoke the fires
of hell they've brought to earth.

I have searched for God continuously
through sacred texts in foreign tongues
and empty bottles in empty rooms
I have opened my heart, my spleen, my mind
standing naked begging a sign.
It is not redemption that I ask,

only recognition,
God,
simply recognition.

II.
On some levels
I consider myself the luckiest man alive.
I love my wife Caroline and
children Casey and Levi dearly
and unconditionally with all
the power of my being.
I believe they love and respect me
in return for who I am
and protecting them from
loneliness, materialism
and small-town Jersey thinking.

The students I teach in high school
seem to enjoy spending time with me,
(I know I like spending time with them)
and most are willing to work either
for themselves, or to please me
though they think me quaint,
and a throwback to another time
that they cannot quite place.

I am fighting a successful war
against encroaching middle age
bitterness, though of late
my resolve has weakened,
manifest in my begrudging and curmudgeoning
younger folks their due
for digging through the steaming
dung heaps our collective culture
buries us in with shovelfuls

of ignoramus radio, eBay, MTV,
and previewed news
we're permitted to see and read.
I salute all the crazy bastards
who spit when they speak of society
that wants to mold us into corporate
dry-cleaned drones
following the scent of money
like lemmings over the cliff.
If I sound bitter, remember I'm not.
I'm just a lonely battle-weary soldier
fighting a never-ending war.

I have lived to see a pope ask forgiveness
for the persecution of my people.
For what it's worth,
in the name of my father and mother,
I forgive
but I'll never forget.

I still believe in the promised land
and I believe the promise is here
not milk and honey
nor guns and money
the promise is here
it begins with love
We can be the chosen people
if only we can choose ourselves
(I don't know exactly how to say this poetically but:)
We got to take from the rich and
then take some more and
We got to take from the rich and
then take some more and
then we got to take from the rich
and take some more

until they understand
how lucky they are
to live on our land.
We can take back the future
give it to our children to hold.

I can find beauty
in most anything:
a 7-year-old's toothless smile,
Elizabeth Taylor's aging violet eyes,
Jersey Turnpike sunset
on a mid-September night,
earthworms squirming
on a Harlem sidewalk in the rain,
my childbearing wife
screaming through the pain.
Beauty is the beholder.

The journey may be
in the middle
or is about to end
or has just begun
it doesn't matter
it's not about me
it's all about me
and the truth I see
and the truth that I be
and what I believe
and what I invent
what it means to be
middle-aged me.

Invitation to Walt

—for Occupy Wall Street

From Camden come, rise from the dust
fly to Zuccotti Park with your shaggy beard
and your old school hat come see what's happened
to your home and your beloved democracy.

Let's grab a beer or eight at McSorley's
your old haunt, where 19th-century dirt clings
to chandeliers, let's reminisce and plan
our trek through New York's teeming streets

before we saunter to the Bowery or the Nuyorican
where exclaimers and exhorters still sling verse
of hope and despair to hungry crowds who
still believe in the power of the word.

We need your sweeping vision, Walt,
to offer our children more than low expectations
of life sat in front of screens or held in gadgets
that promise expression, but offer convention.

Let us not see America through rose-colored
blinders, but as it is, an unfinished kaleidoscopic
cacophony created by imperfect human hands,
beautiful in complexion, ghastly in reflection.

This new century has been cruel and unusual,
the ideology of greed consuming itself in a spasm
of defeat engineered by merchants of fear
and postmillennial prophets of doom.

We need to recognize healthcare
and education as basic human rights,
we need to restore the dignity of work
as well as the dignity of leisure from work.

We need to get off our flabby asses
to dance as if nobody is watching, to howl
to stir shit up, to worry the rich
with a real threat of class warfare.

We need to take back our democracy, from the masters of Wall Street,
banks too big to fail, insurance deniers, education profiteers,
from closet racists, and self-appointed homophobes,
the unholy trinity of greed, corruption, and cruelty.

Walt, give me the courage to not be scared
to offend, to tell the truth which is:
most Republicans are heartless bastards
more willing to sink our elected head of state

to protect the interests of the moneyed
than do what's right for the greater good.
They are the party that has impeded progress
and sucked the joy out of any forward movement

for all my 54 years and they've only gotten more sour,
they scare me with their fascist posturing
while most Democrats are frightened
as usual to betray the welfare of the rich

(Historians of the future will laugh at us).

Yet, we've come so far in so many ways,
call it evolutionary progress if you will
though there's so much work left undone.
We need a revolutionary spirit to unfold.

It's time for us to dream big again
of democratic vistas and barbaric yawps
of space travel and scientific discovery
where we protect our glorious habitat

and build structures worthy of our dreams.
Imagine America based on empathy and equality
where we lend a hand to those in need
unembarrassed to embrace our ideals.

Walt, we're here, citizen poets for change
across the United States and we believe,
we believe, call us dreamers, call us fools,
call us the dispossessed, your children lost,

our hopes on hold, left no choice but to stand
our backs against the corporate wall
ready to fight for what we're owed,
for what we've worked, promises bought and sold.

Let your spirit rise, old Walt Whitman
take us with you to another place and time
remind us what is good about ourselves
basic decency that's been forgotten

May your words guide our daydreams of deliverance
let the hijacked past tumble away
let the dismal present state be but a blip
may the undecided future begin today

let us become undisguised and naked
let us walk the open road . . .

Acknowledgments

Thanks to the editors of the following publications in which versions of some of these poems first appeared: *Long Shot, Aloud: Voices from the Nuyorican Poets Café, The Outlaw Bible of American Poetry, Live Mag, Five:2:One Magazine, Gambazine, Horizons.*

Special Thanks: Eliot Katz, Robert Press, Nancy Mercado, Teresa Carson, Tim Ree, Andy Clausen, Jack Wiler, Joel Lewis, Hersch Silverman, Alicia Ostriker, Pedro Pietri, Chavisa Woods, Steve Cannon, Reg E. Gaines, Paul Beatty, Jeanne Beaumont, Joan Cusack Handler and the CavanKerry Staff, and the whole *Long Shot* Crew.

CavanKerry's Mission

CavanKerry Press is committed to expanding the reach of poetry to a general readership by publishing poets whose works explore the emotional and psychological landscapes of everyday life.

Other Books in the Florenz Eisman Memorial Series

Abloom & Awry, Tina Kelley

WORKS was designed by Mayfly Design, and set in Source Sans Pro, a grotesque sans serif font created by Paul D. Hunt for Adobe in 2012.